FOR YOUR HOME

PORCHES & SUNROOMS

For Your Home

Porches & Sunrooms

Jessica Elin Hirschman

Little, Brown and Company
Boston   Toronto   London

DEDICATION

FOR MY GRANDMOTHER, MOLLIE ELIN, IN HONOR OF HER HIGH-RISE APARTMENT PATIO AND ITS SWEEPING VIEW OF BOTH CITY AND NATURE.

ACKNOWLEDGMENTS

MANY THANKS TO THE HOMEOWNERS, ARCHITECTS, AND INTERIOR DESIGNERS WHO GRACIOUSLY TOOK TIME TO ANSWER QUESTIONS ABOUT THEIR WORK. I ALSO WISH TO EXPRESS MY GRATITUDE TO THE FOLLOWING PEOPLE, COMPANIES, AND ASSOCIATIONS FOR THEIR ENTHUSIASTIC ASSISTANCE IN THE RESEARCHING AND PRODUCTION OF THIS BOOK: AMDEGA/MACHIN CONSERVATORIES; THE AMERICAN INSTITUTE OF ARCHITECTS; ROBERT DAVIS OF SEASIDE IN FLORIDA; FOUR SEASONS SUNROOMS; THE MICHAEL FRIEDMAN GROUP; THE SOCIETY OF ARCHITECTURAL HISTORIANS.

Copyright © 1993 by Michael Friedman Publishing Group, Inc.

First Edition

ISBN 0-316-36466-5

Library of Congress Catalogue Card Number 92-56183

A FRIEDMAN GROUP BOOK

10 9 8 7 6 5 4 3 2 1

Published simultaneously in Canada by Little, Brown & Company (Canada) Limited

FOR YOUR HOME: PORCHES & SUNROOMS
was prepared and produced by
Michael Friedman Publishing Group, Inc.
15 West 26th Street
New York, New York 10010

Editor: Dana Rosen
Designer: Lynne Yeamans
Art Director: Jeff Batzli
Photography Editor: Christopher C. Bain
Production Director: Karen Matsu Greenberg

Color separations by Bright Arts (Singapore) Pte. Ltd.
Printed and bound in Hong Kong by Leefung-Asco Printers Ltd.

Grateful acknowledgment is given to architects, designers, and photographers. Every effort has been made to correctly credit contributors to the projects. In the case of any omissions, the publishers will be pleased to make suitable acknowledgments in future editions.

Table of Contents

INTRODUCTION

Historically, porches and sunrooms have enjoyed a unique status in residential architecture, bridging the gap between unbounded open space and protected shelter. Today, as the pace of life accelerates and neighborhoods become more and more crowded, a need for open, private living spaces intensifies. The nineties have witnessed a worldwide heightened awareness of the environment, and accompanying this consciousness is a desire to feel a part of nature whenever possible. Porches and sunrooms — transition spaces between inside and outside — address all these desires. These structures, with a long history in residential design, are now undergoing a newfound popularity.

Porches are also called verandas and porticos. Although there are architectural differences among these structures, in the vernacular the terms are generally used interchangeably. Strictly speaking, a porch is

a sheltered entrance, usually a principal entrance, that is permanently attached to and projecting from a building. A veranda is an open, galley-like structure with its own roof and is positioned along the side of a house but not necessarily at its main entrance. Verandas are larger than porches, generally extending the length of the primary elevation and often wrapping around to one or two sides of a house. The word *veranda* came from the Portuguese language via India and entered the Western design lexicon through England.

Left: IN THIS CONVERTED ARTIST'S STUDIO, THE SEPARATION BETWEEN INSIDE AND OUTSIDE IS AS SUBTLE AS THE GREEN SILK CURTAIN THAT OUTLINES THE THRESHOLD AND COMPLEMENTS THE ROOM'S RICH GOTHIC OVERTONES. A GRASS MATTING TREATMENT ON THE CEILING WINDOWS SHIELDS THE HANDWOVEN TAPESTRY UPHOLSTERY FROM LIGHT AND DISGUISES THE ROUGH WOOD WINDOW FRAMES. THE CONCRETE FLOOR, SCORED TO RESEMBLE LARGE BRICKS, IS FRESHLY PAINTED AND STENCILED FOR A FORMAL, FINISHED LOOK. Above: HISTORICALLY, THE DESIGN AND FURNISHING OF A FRONT PORCH WAS AN INTEGRAL STRUCTURAL AND AESTHETIC ELEMENT OF A HOME'S FAÇADE. THE PILLARS OF THIS PORCH REFLECT THE INFLUENCE OF GREEK REVIVAL ARCHITECTURE. THE ELEVATED SEATING AREA IS FURNISHED IN A POPULAR COUNTRY STYLE.

Porticos are long, formal, symmetrical porches derived from classical Greek architecture. The portico is protected overhead by a triangular gable or pediment roofline that is supported by columns. Porticos traditionally were designed to shelter main entrances but over time were moved to the sides of buildings, especially churches, to protect secondary entrances and egresses.

Originally, one of the primary functions of the porch was to help cool a house. In warm climates where passive solar cooling was essential, homes often featured a second-story porch to allow the circulation of breezes. Extensive roof overhangs also helped cool interior rooms by shading the porch. And on very hot nights, the porch often doubled as a makeshift bedroom.

Particularly in warm climates, the function of the porch was expanded into the social arena (in cold, less hospitable regions, it functioned mainly as temporary shelter from inclement weather). As porches grew in size and boasted more elaborate designs, they became gathering spots and served as prime vantage points over daily neighborhood happenings or surrounding vistas. In agrarian societies, porches often formed the dividing line between work (outside) and play (inside). These in-between spaces were the resting place for dirty shoes and work clothes.

Once air conditioning became widespread, porches were slowly abandoned in favor of cooler, more comfortable interiors. Today, however, residential design is witnessing a revival of the porch. A growing fondness for homes that strike a nostalgic chord is causing many people to return to architecture reminiscent of their

Above: IN COLD CLIMATES, PORCHES OFFER TEMPORARY RESPITE FROM INCLEMENT WEATHER. THIS SHED-STYLE PORCH ON A STONE CABIN ALSO PROVIDES DRY, ACCESSIBLE FIREWOOD STORAGE. TABLE AND CHAIRS ALLOW THE PORCH TO BE FULLY ENJOYED ON WARM DAYS.

parents' or grandparents' homes. For some, that might mean the inclusion of a front or back porch; for others it entails a different type of indoor/outdoor space such as a sunroom or conservatory.

By definition, a sunroom is a room that receives a lot of sun; it might be a freestanding, all-glass structure or an enclosed porch with floor-length windows and sky-lights. Although *solarium, sun space,* and *conservatory* are all commonly accepted terms for sunrooms, there are differences between a sunroom and an authentic English-style conservatory.

The term *conservatory* dates back to England in the eighteenth century, when "conservative walls" were erected to facilitate the growing of fruit. These walls were actually the combination of two separate struc-tures, one solid — most likely brick or stone — and the other a frame of glass that was placed a few feet in front of the solid wall. The resulting narrow, partially sheltered plot of land became the fruit garden. The con-cept of the conservatory as an independent structure, however, is even older.

Botanical gardens, extremely popular in sixteenth-century Europe, arrived in England around the year 1620 but did not weather the British climate very well. By the end of the century, an inspired gardener had come up with the idea of constructing a glass building to harbor the delicate plants through the winter months. As the British developed a penchant for exotic fruits such as lemons and oranges, these seasonal havens became known as orangeries. Generally composed of a glass roof and glass wall panels, orangeries were used to dis-play and cultivate the tender fruit plants, and eventually heating and lighting systems were added to better control the indoor climate. Edwardians appropriately termed the glass structures "winter gardens."

Conservatories came into their own architecturally, too. Designing and constructing glass buildings was ele-vated to an art form, and ornamentation signifying wealth and stature became the conservatory's hallmark. Conservatories not only housed horticulture; they extended the living space and brought light into England's interiors during damp winter months.

In terms of both design and popularity, the English conservatory achieved its apogee in the late nineteenth century, but with a growing disfavor of things Victorian suffered a decline during the early twentieth century. But these unique buildings would endure and enjoy newfound popularity in and far beyond England in later years.

Residential design for the 1990s is moving back to basics. Sunrooms and conservatories make it possible to live close to nature and create a sense of openness without compromising the need to be protected and sheltered. These structures are an economical way to improve a home, as they are viable for use as breakfast rooms, home offices, or mini-kitchens. They can also be designed to serve as a breezeway between garage and house or to link an existing structure to an addition.

Topping a townhouse with a conservatory will add a bonus floor of warm, accessible living space.

How the sun space is used may determine its position. Southern exposures are best for capturing the most daylight but may be too hot in warm climates. In cool regions, siting a conservatory on a true east-west axis will allow it to collect heat throughout most of the day. Aligning the structure with a specific view is also an option. A conservatory or sunroom must be able to withstand local weather, and how it will be used will determine its heating, cooling, and lighting systems.

The following chapters contain beautiful examples of porches, sunrooms, and other spaces that, although technically neither porch nor sunroom, illustrate the extent to which architecture can reconcile the need for shelter with the desire for open space.

Right: TRADITIONAL ENGLISH CONSERVATORIES BEGAN AS WINTER HARBORS FOR DELICATE, EXOTIC FRUITS AND HAVE EVOLVED INTO LIVING AREAS THAT STRIKE A GRACIOUS BALANCE BETWEEN INDOOR AND OUTDOOR SPACE. THE GLAMOROUS INTERIOR OF THIS FREESTANDING CONSERVATORY WAS CAREFULLY DESIGNED TO REFLECT AND REFRACT LIGHT. A FACETED CHANDELIER BOUNCES THE SUN'S RAYS ACROSS THE VAULTED GLASS CEILING, WHILE SILVER-LEAFED GLASS CABOCHONS REFLECT LIGHT UPWARD FROM THE ELEGANT FLOOR. EVEN THE SKIRTING OF THE TERRY CLOTH RECLINING SOFA POSSESSES TINY, DAZZLING CRYSTALS. THE CLASSICALLY STYLED CHAIR AND EARLY NINETEENTH-CENTURY BRONZE TABLE BRING THE EXCLUSIVE ELEGANCE OF AN ITALIAN PALACE TO THIS GARDEN HIDEAWAY (EXTERIOR VIEW PAGE 36).

PORCHES

"The porch is a great social device," explains Robert Davis, developer of Seaside, a planned community in Florida that seeks to recapture the bygone era of small-town living. "Even it unoccupied, porches present a friendly face to the street." Elizabeth Plater-Zyberk, who along with partner Andres Duany developed the master town plan for Seaside, points out that porches are occupants' connection to the street. "On a porch it's possible to be in a private space and still participate in a public sense — and the public can participate in a home-owner's private world."

The boundaries between private and public realms can be intentionally blurred by the design of a porch. Architectural details or furnishings often set the tone of the space, just as design and decoration establish the mood of an interior room. Not only is the porch an extension of the living spaces, it is often the first element of a home that visitors see. The following photographs present ideas for enjoying the private, the public, the formal, and the relaxed pleasures of a porch.

Left: THE RENTAL HONEYMOON COTTAGES AT THE PLANNED COMMUNITY OF SEASIDE, FLORIDA, FEATURE TWO DISTINCT PORCHES. THE GROUND-LEVEL PORCH, WHICH CONNECTS TO THE BEDROOM, IS SCREENED IN FOR PRIVACY. THE SECOND-STORY PORCH OFF THE LIVING ROOM IS OPEN TO TAKE ADVANTAGE OF THE STUNNING VISTA. THESE DOUBLE-STORY PORCHES ARE CAPPED WITH A GALVANIZED METAL ROOF AND HAVE WOOD FLOORING THAT HAS BEEN BLEACHED FOR A COOL, FRESH LOOK. Above left: THE SLIGHT OPENING BETWEEN THE RAILING AND PORCH FLOOR FACILITATES THE DRYING OF THE WOOD AFTER RAIN. Above right: ARCHITECT LEON KRIER'S HOME AT SEASIDE IS A FOUR-STORY TOWERLIKE STRUCTURE WITH SEVERAL PORCHES. THE RAILING IS A UNIQUE DESIGN BUT THE EXPOSED RAFTER CEILING MATCHES THOSE OF SURROUNDING PORCHES.

Above: A PORTICO PAYS HOMAGE TO ITS GREEK HERITAGE WITH A CONTEMPORARY TWIST. FINE ROUND COLUMNS FRAME THE DOOR IN A CLASSICAL MANNER, BUT THEIR ASYMMETRICAL PLACEMENT ADDS A SURPRISING, DISTINCTIVE RHYTHM TO THE HOME'S FRONT FAÇADE. **Right:** REMINISCENT OF A GREEK TEMPLE, THE COLUMNED PORCH ON THIS PRIVATE RESIDENCE IS TECHNICALLY A VERANDA BECAUSE IT EXTENDS BEYOND THE HOME'S ENTRANCE; VERANDAS GENERALLY RUN THE LENGTH OF A FRONT ELEVATION AND WRAP AROUND THE SIDE OF A HOUSE. OFTEN, HOWEVER, LOCAL VERNACULAR RATHER THAN ADHERENCE TO ARCHITECTURAL DEFINITIONS DETERMINES THE POPULAR NAME OF A PORCH. THE ABSENCE OF RAILINGS MAKES THIS PORCH FEEL EVEN MORE OPEN AND SPACIOUS.

Far left: ON THIS PORCH, A CASUAL COMBINATION OF COLOR, STYLE, AND FLORA ENHANCES A SHINGLE-STYLE HOME. CHINTZ PILLOWS AND A HANDCRAFTED RUG DECORATE THE ARRANGEMENT IN EASY-GOING COMFORT. **Top left:** A CAREFUL BALANCE OF INDOOR AND OUTDOOR ELEMENTS GIVES THIS PORCH A WELCOMING SPIRIT. THE INCORPORATION OF SIDE-BY-SIDE SKYLIGHTS AND THE PREDOMINANT USE OF WHITE—INCLUDING AN OFF-WHITE AREA RUG PLACED ATOP THE WHITE-PAINTED FLOORBOARDS—UNIFY THE SPACE AND MAKE IT FEEL LIKE AN INTIMATE LIVING ROOM. **Bottom left:** BLUE STAIRS AND FLOOR, WHICH FEATURES A HAND-PAINTED OLD-FASHIONED COMPASS, MAKE THIS BACK-DOOR PORTICO EVOCATIVE OF A FRONT PORCH FROM THE 1920S. THE SOLID-BLUE ACCENT PILLOWS APPEAR TUFTED BUT ARE ACTUALLY TROMPE L'OEIL CHINTZ.

Above: SCULPTED RAILS HARMONIZE WITH GREEK COLUMNS, BEFITTING THE PALATIAL FEEL OF A PORCH WITH A COMMANDING VIEW. **Near right:** THE PORCH OF THIS HILLSIDE CABIN FEATURES A CUSTOM-DESIGNED RAILING THAT ECHOES THE SHAPE OF THE SURROUNDING TREES. THE RAILING'S BROWN-STAINED "BRANCHES" TOPPED WITH GREEN REINFORCE THE IMAGE. BOTH THE RAILING AND WAVY PINE CHAIRS RECALL THE TURN-OF-THE-CENTURY ARTS AND CRAFTS DESIGN MOVEMENT. **Far right:** A CLASSIC RAILING ON A PORCH IN CARILLON, FLORIDA, REFLECTS THE REGIONAL CREOLE STYLE OF ARCHITECTURE. THE RAILING CAP IS SLIGHTLY SLOPED, AS IS THE FLOOR, TO FACILITATE WATER RUNOFF.

Below: BOYER AND JOHNSON WORKED TEN YEARS ON THE PROJECT, SELECTING KILN-DRIED RED-WOOD FOR THE STRUCTURAL ELEMENTS, INCLUDING THE BALUSTRADES AND NEWEL POSTS OF THE FRONT STAIRS. Right: THE SECOND-STORY GABLE, WHICH WAS BADLY CHARRED IN THE FIRE, WAS REPRODUCED RIGHT DOWN TO THE HORSESHOE-SHAPED ARCH THAT WAS THE FASHION AT THE TIME THE HOUSE WAS BUILT. A NEW, HISTORICALLY CORRECT FINIAL CROWNS THE TURRET SHELTERING THE LEFT END OF THE PORCH.

INTRICATE, ELABORATE PORCHES WERE A HALLMARK OF VICTORIAN STICK-STYLE AND QUEEN ANNE HOMES. THIS GRAND EXAMPLE OF QUEEN ANNE ECLECTIC IS ACTUALLY A COMPLETE RENOVATION, PAINSTAKINGLY UNDERTAKEN BY HOMEOWNERS JUDY BOYER AND JOE JOHNSON AFTER A FIRE DESTROYED THE HOME'S SECOND STORY. Above: A PHOTO-GRAPH FROM THE INTERIOR OF THE PORCH PROVIDES A CLOSE VIEW OF THE REFURBISHED ORIGINAL LATTICEWORK AND THE MOON ARCHES—A DETAIL THAT BOYER BELIEVES WAS DERIVED FROM THE INFLUENCE OF THE ORIENTAL SHIPPING TRADE. THE STRAIGHT-GRAIN CEDAR FLOORING WAS PAINTED AN AUTHENTIC SHADE OF GRAY, WHILE THE WILLIAMSBURG BLUE CEILING IS IN KEEPING WITH PHOTOGRAPHS FROM THE PERIOD.

Left: AN EXAGGERATED OVERHANG ADDS A DEFINITE SENSE OF ENCLOSURE TO THIS PORCH. THE RED AND YELLOW STRIPES SET OFF THE CEILING AND CREATE THE ILLUSION OF A PARTIAL WALL.

Below: THIS UNUSUALLY LARGE, ROUND PORCH IS THE PERFECT SETTING FOR PAMPERED INDOOR/OUTDOOR LIVING. THE FABRIC-WRAPPED CEILING, BALLOON SHADES, AND FORMAL DRAPES MAKE THE ROOM FEEL LIKE A ROMANTIC, CANOPIED CAROUSEL. THE VIEW, THE POTTED PLANTS, AND THE WICKER FURNITURE ARE THE ONLY REMINDERS THAT THIS IS A PORCH. SEE-THROUGH PLASTIC SHEETS SHELTER THE ROOM FROM THE ELEMENTS BUT CAN BE RAISED TO LET IN AIR.

DECORATING A PORCH CAN BE AS PERSONAL AS ACCESSORIZING ANY OTHER PART OF THE HOUSE. DIFFERENT ROOF STRUCTURES AND CEILING TREATMENTS HELP SHAPE THE CHARACTER OF THESE PORCHES.

Left: EXPOSED HARDWOOD RAFTERS APPEAR NATURAL AND UNPRETENTIOUS ON THIS PORCH WITH MINIMAL DETAILS. THE PITCHED ROOF HELPS SHADE THE PORCH, WHILE LOUVERED DOORS ALLOW BREEZES TO CIRCULATE THROUGH THE ADJACENT INTERIOR SPACES WITHOUT COMPROMISING PRIVACY.

Top right: ARTFUL INTERPRETATIONS OF TIMELESS ADIRONDACK CHAIRS SUIT THE CONTEMPORARY FEEL OF THIS COLORFUL FLAGSTONE PATIO. THE RANDOM, UNEVENLY SHAPED BURSTS OF RED, GRAY, AND BLUE CONTRAST WITH THE STUCCO HOUSE, MAKING THE PATIO FLOOR APPEAR AS WALL-TO-WALL PATTERNED CARPET.

Bottom right: FURNITURE CAN ESTABLISH THE PERSONALITY OF AN OUTDOOR SPACE. HERE, A RUSTIC TABLE AND CHAIRS SET THE MOOD FOR ALFRESCO DINING ON AN ELEVATED PORCH. THE FURNISHINGS ARE PATTERNED AFTER THE TWIG FURNITURE MADE POPULAR IN THE AMERICAN SOUTH—IT WAS MOST OFTEN CONSTRUCTED OF HICKORY BECAUSE OF THE WOOD'S EXCEPTIONAL ABILITY TO WEATHER HEAT AND HUMIDITY. UPHOLSTERED THROW PILLOWS CUSHION THE SLAT SEATS AND COMPLEMENT THE VINE-WRAPPED CORNERPOSTS AND RAILING.

Right: AT THE OPPOSITE END OF THE ABOVE PORCH, A WICKER SETTEE AND OVERSIZED ARMCHAIR WITH A WARM TOBACCO FINISH PROVIDE THE PERFECT OUTDOOR GROUPING FOR A CASUAL CONVERSATION OR AFTERNOON TEA. THE HOOKED RUG AND WICKER TRUNK USED AS A COFFEE TABLE GIVE THE PORCH A LIVED-IN FEELING.

BUILT AS PART OF AN ADDITION TO THE NORTH SIDE OF THIS 1920S HOUSE, THIS PORCH FUNCTIONS AS A NATURALLY COOL LIVING SPACE IN THE SUMMERTIME.

Left: ARRANGED TO MIMIC AN ORIENTAL RUG, THE BLUE AND GREEN TILES OF THE FAMILY ROOM FLOOR REFLECT THE NATURAL PALETTE SURROUNDING THE HOME. SKYLIGHTS HELP DISTRIBUTE LIGHT EVENLY THROUGHOUT THE PORCH.

Right: THIS ELEVATED PORCH HAS THE FEEL OF A TREEHOUSE. LATTICEWORK BETWEEN THE SUPPORTS CREATES THE ILLUSION OF A FLOATING PORCH.

Left: THE USE OF PLYWOOD CUTOUTS WAS A POPULAR DESIGN TECHNIQUE IN THE ARTS AND CRAFTS MOVEMENT OF THE EARLY TWENTIETH CENTURY. HERE, MATISSE- AND ARP-INSPIRED SHAPES CAST DYNAMIC, EVOCATIVE PATTERNS OF SHADOW AND LIGHT ACROSS THE FLOOR.

Right: EXQUISITELY FINISHED HARDWOOD FLOORING, VARNISHED TO WITHSTAND INCLEMENT WEATHER, MAKES THIS SIZABLE PORCH FEEL MORE LIKE A LIVING ROOM THAN AN OUTDOOR SITTING SPACE. THE FULL-SIZE CUSHIONED COUCH AND MATCHING SIDE CHAIRS GIVE THE SPACE A COORDINATED, FURNISHED APPEARANCE. AN ABUNDANCE OF GERANIUMS AND POTTED PLANTS ARE REMINDERS THAT THIS SPACE IS INDEED OUTSIDE.

FLOORING MATERIALS ARE EFFECTIVE DESIGN TOOLS FOR PERSONALIZING A PORCH AND BLURRING THE BOUNDARIES BETWEEN INTERIOR AND EXTERIOR SPACE. **Above:** THE PATTERN OF LARGE GREEN AND WHITE FLOOR TILES SHOWN HERE WOULD BE EQUALLY APPROPRIATE IN A GRAND FOYER. THIS RAMBLING, WELL-SHADED VERANDA RECALLS THOSE OF THE CARIBBEAN, WITH THE CHIPPENDALE-INSPIRED, CUSTOM-DESIGNED CHAIR AND SETTEE GIVING IT A TIMELESS ELEGANCE. THE RAILING IS COMPRISED OF VASE-SHAPED, PRECAST CONCRETE BALUSTERS; SMALLER, SCALED-DOWN VERSIONS COULD EASILY ADORN AN INTERIOR STAIRCASE. **Right:** SIMPLE, NATURAL MATERIALS ARE PERFECT FOR PORCHES WITH A VIEW. TERRA-COTTA TILES AND WOOD SUPPORTS PAINTED A RICH GREEN GIVE THIS PORCH AN ORGANIC FEEL THAT SUITS THE ROLLING AUSTRALIAN LANDSCAPE.

As a quiet place for introspection, a porch can carry people away to another time and place. The right appointments can transport one to a world of opulence and indulgence. **Left:** This sumptuous porch features weather-resistant materials and furnishings, and an exquisite handwoven hammock from South America. The custom trompe l'oeil painting on the plaster ceiling, the rich floor tiles, and the white sailcloth drapes bordered with green-and-white striped diamonds give the porch the quality of a finished indoor room. By contrast, matching statues and flowering plants befitting a formal garden add an outdoor, botanical air. **Above:** Although distinctively set apart by its grand rotunda shape and elegantly stenciled floor, this porch appears to be connected to the lawn by virtue of the shared colors. Green and white curtains sewn from the same fabric that covers the wrought-iron chairs bring a soft sense of enclosure and cohesiveness to the space. Small touches, such as tasseled pull cords and fanciful wrought-iron planters, add to the formal character of the space.

SUNROOMS AND CONSERVATORIES

Sunrooms and conservatories recall a different place and time, a romantic era when house and garden came together within a room of glass. Originally developed in Britain to sustain the growth of exotic fruits, these glass structures were soon filled with varieties of lush foliage and inviting furnishings.

Today, these structures are enhanced by climate-control technologies and construction materials. The development of energy-efficient thermal glass, ultraviolet-reflective window coverings, attractive heat-absorbing tiles, and fade-resistant upholstery has made it feasible to open all homes to the outside.

Architecturally, the distinction between true conservatories and sunrooms is by some accounts subtle and by others great. The difference lies in the roof. Traditional conservatory roofs come in three architectural styles: the ogee, which is an S-shape crowned with a finial; the vault, which resembles a slightly arched dome; and the classic gable roof design. Sunroom roofs, by contrast, are often designed to blend with the roofline of the house rather than stand apart as a distinct architectural structure. Furthermore, traditional conservatories were constructed entirely of glass, whereas the modern-day sunroom can incorporate other building materials.

The photos featured on the following pages present the warm, welcoming world of many types of glass-room additions.

Left: THE BRIGHT PINK, UNIQUELY SHAPED BALCONY AND CIRCULAR STAIRWELL OF THIS GLASS-AND-STEEL-TOPPED SITTING ROOM GIVE THE IMPRESSION THAT IT IS OUTSIDE. INDUSTRIAL OUTDOOR LIGHTING, FRENCH DOORS TRIMMED WITH LACE CURTAINS, AND THE PRESENCE OF THE SKY, VISIBLE THROUGH THE GLASS ROOF, REINFORCE THE IMAGE OF AN EXTERIOR FAÇADE. **Above:** ORIGINALLY A GREENHOUSE, THIS TRADITIONAL ENGLISH CONSERVATORY HAS BEEN CONVERTED INTO AN ARTIST'S STUDIO. IT NOW FEATURES MANUALLY CONTROLLED CANVAS SHADES FOR ADJUSTING THE LIGHTING AND MINIMIZING SOLAR BUILDUP ON HOT AFTERNOONS.

Above: THE INTERIOR OF THIS WHITE-FRAMED CONSERVATORY HAS BEEN ADROITLY FURNISHED BY THE HOMEOWNER, AN ANTIQUES DEALER AND CONSUMMATE FURNITURE COLLECTOR. WINDOWS CAN BE OPENED AND CLOSED INDEPENDENTLY TO DIRECT THE FLOW OF AIR THROUGH THE SPACE OR BREAK A HARSH WIND. **Left:** THE SMALL TRELLIS IS AN ATTRACTIVE, UNOBTRUSIVE WAY TO WRAP THE QUAINT SPACE IN GREENERY. **Right:** INSIDE THE CONSERVATORY, THE VIVID YELLOW WALL REFLECTS SUNLIGHT, MAKING THE SMALL ROOM APPEAR LARGER AND BRIGHTER.

Left: CREAM SILK JACQUARD CURTAINS SWAGGED GENTLY ACROSS THE WINDOWS GIVE THIS VAULTED CONSERVATORY A MYSTERIOUS ALLURE. DELICATE TOPIARY CHAIRS ON EITHER SIDE OF THE INVITING ENTRANCE ADD TO THE ENCHANTMENT (INTERIOR VIEW ON PAGE 11). **Above:** SET AGAINST THE EVENING SKY AND BACKLIT BY AN ADJACENT ROOM, THIS ROUND CONSERVATORY RESEMBLES A ROMANTIC, GLASS-ENCLOSED VICTORIAN PARLOR OR A JEWEL BOX CROWNED WITH A FINIAL.

Above: SUNROOMS ARE PARTICULARLY POPULAR IN COLD CLIMATES, WHERE THE WEATHER PROHIBITS YEAR-ROUND OUTDOOR LIVING. BENT WILLOW AND OTHER COLONIAL FURNISHINGS ARE JUST RIGHT FOR A SUNROOM ADDITION TO A STONE FARMHOUSE. **Right:** IN SOME REGIONS, SUNROOMS ARE SYNONYMOUS WITH SOLARIUMS; BOTH ARE GLASSED-IN ROOMS EXPOSED TO THE SUN. THIS ALUMINUM-FRAMED SOLARIUM CONTAINS A FULLY EQUIPPED KITCHEN WITH DINING AREA FOR YEAR-ROUND "OUTDOOR" ENTERTAINING. SMALLER WINDOWS NEAR THE GOURMET RANGE OPEN TO VENTILATE THE SPACE.

ALTHOUGH NOT PREDOMINANTLY ENCLOSED BY GLASS, THESE LOVELY ROOMS STILL FEEL OPEN TO NATURE. **Above:** ISRAELI SCULPTRESS ILANA GOOR'S LIVING ROOM, WITH HIGHLY POLISHED ISRAELI STONE FLOORING AND FURNISHINGS OF HER OWN DESIGN, OVERLOOKS THE MEDITERRANEAN SEA. **Left:** BAMBOO FURNITURE, A HERRINGBONE-PATTERNED BRICK FLOOR, AND PAINTED BRICK WALLS GIVE THIS FULLY ENCLOSED ROOM A CASUAL, OUTDOOR CHARACTER. **Right:** A SPECTACULAR PANORAMIC VIEW IS SEEN THROUGH THE FLOOR-TO-CEILING WINDOWS AND FRENCH DOORS IN THE MAIN ROOM OF THIS WEEKEND HOME.

Left: THIS SMALL CONSERVATORY LOCATED OFF THE LIBRARY OF THE MARK TWAIN HOUSE IN HARTFORD, CONNECTICUT, REFLECTS THE ARCHITECTURAL HERITAGE OF THE CONSERVATORY AS GREENHOUSE. A SIMPLE SHADE IS THE ONLY PHYSICAL BOUNDARY BETWEEN THE TWO ROOMS AND CAN BE EASILY MANEUVERED FROM EITHER SIDE. **Above:** A GLASS CEILING OF A SEMI-ENCLOSED LONDON PORCH GIVES IT THE LOOK AND FEEL OF A CONSERVATORY. BUILT IN EDWARDIAN TIMES, THIS INDOOR/OUTDOOR ROOM SERVES AS AN EXTENSION OF THE MAIN LIVING SPACE. THE CLIMBING VINES TURN THE PORCH INTO A PRIVATE ARBOR.

Left: WRAPAROUND WINDOWS FLOOD THE SMALL SUNROOM WITH LIGHT AND WARMTH THROUGHOUT THE DAY, AND A HIGH SLOPING CEILING MAKES IT FEEL EVEN MORE OPEN AND AIRY. THE SLATE BORDER IS AN ATTRACTIVE, LOW-MAINTENANCE PERIMETER USEFUL FOR WATERING PLANTS. SLATE ALSO PAVES THE PATIO OUTSIDE, CREATING THE ILLUSION OF UNINTERRUPTED SPACE.

Right: THE SALTBOX ROOFLINE OF THIS COLONIAL HOME FACILITATED THE ADDITION OF A SUNROOM AND FLANKING ALCOVES, WHICH HOUSE A WET BAR ON THE RIGHT AND BUILT-IN BOOKSHELVES ON THE LEFT. FRENCH DOORS CONNECT BOTH ENDS OF THE ADDITION TO THE OUTSIDE.

Left: ALTHOUGH STYLED TO LOOK OLD, THE FARMHOUSE IS ACTUALLY NEW, BUILT FROM MATERIALS COLLECTED OVER A TEN-YEAR PERIOD. MOTORIZED AWNINGS ON THE CEILING AND WALLS SHADE THE SUNROOM DURING THE SUMMER.

Right: THIS L-SHAPED SUNROOM, DESIGNED FOR YEAR-ROUND LIVING, FUNCTIONS AS THE SOLE PASSAGEWAY BETWEEN A MANOR HOUSE AND A BARN STRUCTURE, WHICH IS THE HOME'S GREAT ROOM. MEXICAN QUARRY TILES FASHIONABLY CONCEAL A COIL HEATING SYSTEM LOCATED UNDER THE FLOOR, AND VICTORIAN-STYLE VENTS COVER THE AIR CONDITIONING DUCTS LOCATED NEAR THE TRACK LIGHTING. OLD COPPER LANTERNS—EACH ONE DIFFERENT AND ALL ELECTRIFIED—ILLUMINATE THE SPACE AT NIGHT.

Left: A SWEEPING VIEW OF THE INTERIOR REVEALS THE ROOM'S ECLECTIC CHARACTER, REPLETE WITH ENGLISH REGENCY AND GOTHIC FURNISHINGS. THE PROMINENTLY DISPLAYED BIRD CAGE IS AN AUTHENTIC CHINESE CHIPPENDALE-STLYE DESIGN. THE TILED FLOOR AND MOTORIZED CANVAS WINDOW COVERINGS ARE THE ONLY VISIBLE REMINDERS OF MODERN-DAY LIVING.

THIS ELEGANT, INVITING ROOM IS ACTUALLY A ROOFTOP CONSERVATORY. **Left:** LIGHT ENTERS THIS CORNER OF THE ROOM FROM THREE LEVELS: THE GLASS ROOF, THE CEILING-HEIGHT STAINED-GLASS WINDOWS, AND A SMALL FLAT SKYLIGHT POSITIONED DIRECTLY ABOVE THE COUCH. GOTHIC-STYLE TWISTING COLUMNS DEFINE THE COVERED SEATING AREA. **Right:** THE DRAMATIC ENTRYWAY RESEMBLES THAT OF A FORMAL GARDEN, COMPLETE WITH A GATELIKE DOOR, LATTICE-COVERED WALLS, AND ART NOUVEAU STATUES.

OUTDOOR STRUCTURES AND SPACES

Articulating the relationship between interior and exterior, renowned architect Miës Van der Rohe stated: "The window is a wall, a screen, a garden." Swiss-born modern architect Le Corbusier, a master of the manners in which design articulates space, conceptualized space as continuous rather than finite and bounded, considering basic structures such as walls to be mediators, not barriers.

The rooms, structures, and spaces featured on the following pages exemplify how today's architecture interprets the ideas of Van der Rohe, Corbusier, and other innovative architects concerning inside and outside space. The projects all fall under the general heading of "outdoor spaces" but each examines the issue of how to blur boundaries in an individual way.

Some projects take a subtle approach, others strongly deemphasize the traditional definitions of indoor and outdoor. Still others actually invert the concept through the clever use of a cabana, a gazebo, or removable glass panels. They are all included in this book about porches and sunrooms for their ingenuity— and for their ability to reexamine the relationship between shelter and exposure, between indoor and outdoor spaces, and between private and public realms.

Left: BY ESTABLISHING VISUAL AND PHYSICAL BOUNDARIES, OUTDOOR STRUCTURES DEFINE EXTERIOR SPACES JUST AS WALLS DELINEATE INTERIOR ONES. THIS THOUGHTFULLY DESIGNED, OPEN WOOD FRAME CONTRASTS WITH THE SOLIDLY ENCLOSED SPACES OF THE ADJOINING HOUSE. THE STRUCTURE, BUILT FROM DOUGLAS FIR, WAS PAINTED GREEN TO BLEND WITH SURROUNDING FOLIAGE. Above: A BROADLY SCALED TRELLIS SERVES AS A ROOF OF SORTS TO THIS TROPICAL COURTYARD. CARIBBEAN COLORS DECORATE THE SPACE, AND ARCHED PORTALS PROVIDE A GLIMPSE OF THE GARDEN BEYOND.

HERE, AS IN NOMADIC TRADITION, TEXTILES SERVE AS THE ONLY BOUNDARIES SURROUNDING PRIVATE
OUTDOOR LIVING SPACES. **Above:** THE IMAGINATIVE USE OF A SOFTLY PATTERNED PASTEL CURTAIN IN PLACE
OF CONVENTIONAL SCREENS TURNS A SIMPLE DECK INTO A LOVELY BILLOWING HIDEAWAY. OVERSIZED
PILLOWS EVOKE THE AMBIENCE OF A RICHLY APPOINTED ARABIAN TENT. **Right:** THE IMAGINATIVE OWNER OF
THIS HOME TURNED A GARAGE-TOP PATIO INTO A WHIMSICAL ROOM FOR OUTDOOR ENTERTAINING.

Left: THIS GAZEBO, A FRENCH COUNTRY STRUCTURE THAT FEATURES A CEDAR SHAKE ROOF AND DOUGLAS FIR COMPONENTS, WAS ASSEMBLED ON SITE FROM A KIT. **Below:** THE MILLED REDWOOD FLOOR IN THIS PREFABRICATED GAZEBO IS DESIGNED TO LOOK LIKE INDIVIDUAL BRICKS BUT IS ACTUALLY ONE UNIT THAT FOLDS IN HALF FOR EASY INSTALLATION.

A GAZEBO IS A FREESTANDING, ROOFED STRUCTURE THAT IS GENERALLY ROUND OR OCTAGONAL AND IS OPEN ON ALL SIDES. HISTORICALLY, GAZEBOS AND GARDEN HOUSES ENJOYED A UNIQUE STATUS, PARTICULARLY IN FORMAL GARDENS, WHERE THEY FUNCTIONED AS A SPOT FROM WHICH TO APPRECIATE THE COLORFUL, MANICURED SCENERY AND BECAME AN INTEGRAL PART OF THE GARDEN DESIGN. **Left:** THIS ORNATE, CLASSICALLY SHAPED WROUGHT-IRON GAZEBO WAS PURPOSEFULLY PLACED AWAY FROM THE HOUSE TO CREATE A TRANQUIL, SECLUDED SPOT FOR ENJOYING THE STRIKING LANDSCAPE.

LE CORBUSIER, AN INNOVATOR IN THE FIELD OF MODERN ARCHITECTURE, EXPLORED THE RELATIONSHIP

OF INTERIOR AND EXTERIOR SPACES, CONSIDERING WALLS TO BE MEDIATORS BETWEEN SPACES RATHER

THAN IMMUTABLE BARRIERS SEPARATING THEM. THESE OCEANSIDE DECKS, SUBTLY SEPARATED FROM THE

SURROUNDING LAND AND SEA BY GLASS PANELS, CONFORM TO LE CORBUSIER'S CONCEPTUAL FRAMEWORK.

Above: ON HIS OWN REDWOOD DECK, ARCHITECT ANDY NEUMAN INSTALLED TEMPERED GLASS TO

BUFFER THE PREVAILING NORTHWEST WINDS. THE GLASS SCREEN RESEMBLES A SERIES OF WINDOWS

PUNCTUATING A CURVED REDWOOD WALL, AN ILLUSION THAT GIVES THE DECK A MORE ENCLOSED FEEL.

Right: A GLASS WINDBREAK SHELTERS BUILT-IN SEATING ON A DECK DESIGNED FOR BEACHSIDE DINING.

Left: ATOP A MANHATTAN BROWNSTONE, TEXTURED WHITE CANVAS DRAPED OVER A SIMPLE FRAME CREATES A CABANA-STYLE HAVEN FROM THE COMMOTION OF THE CITY BELOW. INSIDE, AN ELEGANT COPPER-FRAME LOUNGE IS STRATEGICALLY POSITIONED TO OVERLOOK THE FRAGRANT CONTAINER GARDEN. **Right:** TUCKED INTO THE CORNER OF THIS SMALL BALCONY, A SIMPLE CHAISE LOUNGE WITH CLASSICAL LINES PROVIDES A RELAXING VANTAGE POINT TO THE SURROUNDING HILLY TERRAIN.

Left: TERRACES FUNCTION AS SMALL OUTDOOR REFUGES WITHIN DENSE URBAN LIVING ENVIRONMENTS, PARTICULARLY WHEN THEY RISE ABOVE NEIGHBORING ROOFTOPS. FEATHEROCK, NATURALLY FORMED BLOCKS OF PUMICE WEIGHING EIGHTY PERCENT LESS THAN GRANITE, IS A LIGHTWEIGHT ALTERNATIVE TO BOULDERS AND A CONVINCING WAY TO BRING THE RURAL COUNTRYSIDE TO THIS CITY SKYDECK.

Left: THIS SMALL PATIO LOCATED OFF A TOWN-HOUSE IS FURNISHED MINIMALLY BUT MEMORABLY. LACY-LOOKING WHITE FURNITURE STANDS OUT AGAINST A BACKGROUND OF NATURAL COLOR, AND A WOODEN WHEELBARROW FUNCTIONS AS A PLANTER. **Below:** THIS PATIO IS SURROUNDED BY A CONCRETE-BLOCK AND WOOD STRUCTURE THAT IS SUGGESTIVE OF A HOUSE UNDER CONSTRUCTION. **Right:** THE IMMENSITY OF THIS OUTDOOR PATIO, PERGOLA, AND FIREPLACE—THE SLATE FLOOR TILES EACH MEASURE 24 INCHES (60CM) SQUARE—SUITS THE PROPORTIONS OF THE EXTENSIVE LAWNS AND TALL TREES BEYOND. THE PERGOLA IS WIRED FOR OUTDOOR LIGHTING.

Left: THE OWNERS OF THIS POOL HOUSE, WHICH IS SEPARATE FROM THEIR MAIN HOUSE, WANTED AN AFTERNOON AROUND THE POOL TO FEEL LIKE A VACATION IN BERMUDA. THE BUILDING FEATURES A COPPER-AND-GLASS VAULTED SKYLIGHT THAT WARMS AND BRIGHTENS THE INTERIOR. **Above left:** THE POOL HOUSE IS COMPLETELY SELF-CONTAINED, WITH A FULLY EQUIPPED KITCHEN, STAGING AREA, AND DINING TABLE.

Above right: THE PALETTE CHOSEN FOR THE POOL HOUSE REFLECTS THE WARM, TROPICAL COLORS OF BERMUDA. THE LIGHT COLORS AND WHIMSICAL FORMS EVOKE A PLAYFUL, RELAXED ATMOSPHERE OF ESCAPE FROM EVERYDAY HUSTLE AND BUSTLE.

Left: AS THE FOCAL POINT OF BACKYARD LIVING, A POOL CAN BECOME A PERSONAL FANTASYLAND. AT THIS PRIVATE ESTATE, WATER FALLS FROM DUCTS IN THE PERGOLA, PAST NAIAD STATUES, AND INTO THE LUXURIOUS POOL. QUARTZ LAMPS HEAT THE DINING AREA, WHICH IS PARTIALLY SHADED BY AN EXTENSION OF THE PERGOLA. **Above:** THE OPEN BREEZEWAY CONNECTING OPPOSITE WINGS OF THIS HOUSE ALSO FUNCTIONS AS AN OUTDOOR DINING ROOM.

Above: THE SLIGHTLY CURVING FORM OF THIS GRAND TERRACE ECHOES ITS MOUNTAINTOP SITE, WHICH AFFORDS A 360-DEGREE VIEW OF THE VALLEY BELOW. IN KEEPING WITH THE EXPANSIVENESS OF THE LAND, LARGE COLUMNS AND AN EQUALLY GENEROUS RAILING ANCHOR THE TERRACE. **Right:** THIS RESIDENCE IN THE CALIFORNIA WINE COUNTRY, WHICH CONFORMS TO THE LOCAL TRADITION OF EXPOSED-WOOD CONSTRUCTION, POSSESSES A WHITE-PAINTED PORCH MODELED AFTER AN OLD-FASHIONED DOG TROT. THE NARROW RUN, INTEGRAL TO THE HOUSE'S TRAFFIC PATTERN, SEPARATES THE LIVING ROOM FROM THE KITCHEN. THE DECK BENEATH THE CEDAR TRUSS AFFORDS A PANORAMIC VIEW OF KNIGHTS VALLEY.

Left: THE TERRACE OF ARCHITECT JOSÉ DE YTURBE'S HOME IN MEXICO REFLECTS REGIONAL DESIGN INFLUENCES AND OFFERS A COMFORTABLE FAMILY RETREAT. A FIREPLACE HOLLOWED OUT FROM ADOBE-COVERED MASONRY WALLS WARMS THE LAKESIDE ROOM. *EQUIPAL* CHAIRS AND STOOLS REPRESENTATIVE OF THE LOCAL STYLE OFFSET CUSHION-COVERED ADOBE BENCHES. **Above:** A RUGGED ROOFTOP TERRACE IN NORTH CAREYES HARBOR, MEXICO, COMPLEMENTS THE ROCKY HEADLAND ON WHICH THE HOUSE SITS. PASTEL WASHES SOFTEN THE PRIMITIVE-LOOKING SPACE, WHILE CUSHIONS AND A BED OF PILLOWS INVITE THE TRAVELER TO PAUSE AND EXPERIENCE THE MAJESTIC CALM OF A MEXICAN SUNSET.

SOURCES

Although not comprehensive, the following resources may be helpful in the construction, preservation, or design of a porch or sunroom. The names of some of the architects and interior designers featured in the book are included. In the interest of space, only their location and phone numbers are provided.

SUNROOMS AND CONSERVATORIES

Amdega/Machin
 Conservatories
P.O. Box 713
Glenview, IL 60025
(708) 729-7212

Four Seasons Solar Products
5005 Veterans Memorial
 Highway
Department C8
Holbrook, NY 11741
(800) 368-7732
(516) 563-4000

Prefabricated Gazebo
JTS Woodworks
18055 Beneda Lane
Canyon Country, CA 91351
(805) 251-0049

BUILDING PRODUCTS/TRADE ASSOCIATIONS

Brick Institute of America
11490 Commerce Park Drive
Reston, VA 22091
(703) 620-0010

Building Stone Institute
Box 507
Purdys, NY 10578
(914) 232-5725

California Redwood
 Association
405 Enfrente Drive
Suite 200
Novato, CA 94949
(415) 382-0662

Featherock, Inc.
20219 Bahama Street
Chatsworth, CA 91311
(818) 882-3888

Industrial Fabrics Association
 International
(awnings and architecture)
305 Cedar Street, Suite 800
St. Paul, MN 55101
(612) 222-2508

Maple Flooring Manufacturers
 Association
60 Revere Drive, Suite 500
Northbrook, IL 60062
(708) 480-9080

Marvin Windows and Doors
P.O. Box 100
Warroad, MN 56763
(800) 346-5128
(800) 552-1167 in Minnesota

National Oak Flooring
 Manufacturers Association
PO Box 3009
Memphis, TN 38173
(901) 526-5016

Resilient Floor Covering
 Institute
966 Hungerford Drive,
 Suite 12B
Rockville, MD 20850
(301) 340-8580

Southern Forest Products
 Association
PO Box 641700
Kenner, LA 70064-1700
(504) 443-4464

Thompsons and Formby
(exterior and interior stains)
825 Crossover Lane
Memphis, TN 38117
(800) 367-6297

Tile Council of America
PO Box 326
Princeton, NJ 08542
(609) 921-7050

Velux Roof Windows and
 Skylights
P.O. Box 5001
Greenwood, SC 29649
(803) 223-8780

Wolman Deck Care Products
Kop-coat Inc.
1824 Koppers Building
436 Seventh Avenue
Pittsburg, PA 15219
(800) 556-7737

ARCHITECTS AND INTERIOR DESIGNERS

(page 6)
Mary Webster Interiors
Princeton, NJ
(609) 921-9168

(page 8)
David Webster & Associates
New York, NY
(212) 924-8932

(pages 11 and 36)
Peter Carlson Design, Inc.
Los Angeles, CA
(213) 969-8423

(page 12)
Scott Merrill, Architect
Vero Beach, Florida
(407) 388-1600

(pages 16, 24, 25)
Sarah Kaltman
New York, NY
(212) 366-9385

(page 17, bottom)
Barbara Southerland Designs
New York, NY
(212) 737-2233
Greenville, NC
(919) 830-1020

(page 18, bottom; pages
    26–27)
Gary Wolf, Architect
Boston, MA
(617) 792-1413

(page 19, top)
Vogt Group Associates
New Orleans, LA
(504) 528-9611

(page 23, top)
Robert DeCarlo Design
    Associates
New York, NY
(212) 245-2968

(page 23, bottom)
Josef Pricci Ltd.
New York, NY
(212) 570-2140

(page 28, top)
Christ Architects and Planners
Point Washington, FL
(904) 231-5538

(page 29)
J. Rolf Seckinger, Inc.
New York, NY
(212) 966-6644

(pages 30 and 46–47)
Barbara Ostrom Associates,
    Inc.
Mahwah, NJ
(201) 529-0444
New York, NY
(212) 465-1808

(page 31
The late Lowell Neas

(page 32)
Michael Davis, Architect
London, England
(071) 407-6574

(page 40, bottom)
The late Rubin deSaaverdra

(page 44)
Kehrt Shatken Sharon
    Architects
Princeton, NJ
(609) 921-1131

(page 48, top)
Gillian Temple Associates/
    Fisons Horticultural Division
Bramford, Ipswich, England
(0473) 830492

(page 50)
Mark Mack, Architect
Santa Monica, CA
(310) 822-0094
San Francisco, CA
(415) 777-5305

(page 51)
Raymond Jungles, ASLA, Inc.
Coconut Grove, FL
(305) 666-9299

(page 53)
Charles Riley
New York, NY
(212) 473-4173
Los Angeles, CA
(213) 383-5838

(page 55)
JTS Woodworks
Canyon Country, CA
(805) 251-0049

(page 56)
Seaside Union Architects
Santa Barbara, CA
(805) 963-4455

(page 57)
Ron Goldman, Architect
Malibu, CA
(310) 456-1831

(page 58)
Vincent Wolf Associates, Inc.
New York, NY
(212) 465-0590

(page 59, right)
Hutton Wilkinson Interior
    Design
Los Angeles, CA
(213) 874-7760

(page 59, left)
Building Stone Institute
Purdys, NY
(914) 232-5725

(pages 61, 64, 66)
Warner Design Associates
San Francisco, CA
(415) 367-9033

(pages 62–63)
Berkus Group Architects
Santa Barbara, CA
(805) 963-8901

(page 67)
William Turnbull Associates
San Francisco, CA
(415) 986-3642

(page 68)
José de Yturbe, Architect
Mexico City, Mexico

(page 69)
Marco Aldaco, Architect
Guadalajara, Mexico

PHOTOGRAPHY CREDITS

© Philip Ennis: 6, 11, 14, 30,
    31, 36, 46, 47 (both)

© Tria Giovan: 7, 16, 17
    (top), 18 (top), 24 (both),
    25, 34 (both), 35, 42, 52

© image/dennis krukowski:
    8, 15, 17 (bottom),
    23 (bottom), 29, 58

© Steven Brooke: 12, 13
    (both), 19, 28 (top), 51, 65

© Gary Wolf Architects: 18
    (bottom)

© David Livingston: 20 (left),
    20 (right), 21, 33, 60
    (right), 61, 64, 66, 67

© Tim Street-Porter: 22, 28
    (bottom), 32, 50, 53, 57,
    59 (left), 68, 69

© Bill Rothschild: 2, 23 (top),
    59 (right)

© Peter Vanderwarker: 26, 27
    (bottom)

© David Hewitt/Anne
    Garrison: 27 (top)

© Marianne Majerus: 37, 43,
    49

© Four Seasons Sunrooms,
    photos by Philip Ennis:
    38, 39

© Peter Paige: 40 (top)

© Daniel Eifert: 40 (bottom)

© Michael Garland: 41, 55
    (both), 56

© Otto Baitz: 44 (both), 45
    (both), 62, 63 (both)

© John Glover: 48 (both), 54,
    60 (left)

INDEX